CRACKING THE CODE

Cheyenne D. Smith

Printed by Prize Publishing House, LLC in the United States of America.

First printing edition 2026.

Prize Publishing House
P.O. Box 9856, Chesapeake, VA 23321
www.PrizePublishingHouse.com

ISBN (Paperback): 979-8-9929954-8-0
ISBN (eBook): 979-8-9929954-9-7

CONTENTS

PREFACE

THE THREAD

Let me tell you something about dreams: they don't die easily. But they can get buried.

I was hanging on by a thread. My environment changed my perspective, and when your perspective shifts in West Philadelphia, the streets don't just call your name—they pull you in by the collar. The dream that started on Easter Sunday, 1990, got pushed to the back of my mind, covered by survival, by choices, by a life that only promised one exit: dirt being thrown on top of everything I was supposed to become.

Incarceration. Twice.

The first time, I told myself it was a mistake. The second time, I was staring down ten years. I served sixteen months, but every day inside, I kept that thread wrapped around my finger. Even when I couldn't see the dream, I never let it go.

They called me "Shoe Foot" on the streets. You know why? Because even in the middle of the chaos, even when I was living a life that should've killed my sense of style, I was still the flyest man out there. I always had the freshest shoes. I always knew what was dropping before anyone else. My perspective had changed, but my fashion? That never left.

Fashion was the thread. And I didn't know it yet, but that thread was connected to something—*Someone*—bigger than me.

THE GARMENT

After my second bid, I went back to my roots. Back to the church. Back to God.

There's a story in scripture about a woman who had been bleeding for twelve years. She'd spent everything she had trying to get healed, and nothing worked. But when she heard Jesus was passing by, she pushed through the crowd, reached out, and touched the hem of His garment. Just the *thread* of His clothing. And she was healed instantly.

That's what happened to me.

It wasn't a lightning bolt moment. It wasn't angels singing. It was quiet. It was the thread of His garment that pulled me out of a life that was designed to destroy me. And when I walked out of those gates and back onto the streets of West Philly, my entire mind had changed.

The original dream came rushing back. The original goal. The original *me*.

I was still in the streets. Still from West Philly. But this time, I was in my own lane. And not only did I never veer off again—I made space for others to see there was another route. Another way. Another exit that didn't end with dirt being thrown on top of their potential.

Fashion saved my life. But more than that, it gave me a way to show others they could be saved too.

EASTER SUNDAY 1990

Philadelphia Zoo. Easter Sunday. 1990.

The air smelled like fresh cut grass, candy, and possibility. Every kid in West Philly knew what Easter Sunday meant— this wasn't just church clothes, this was your *moment*. The day you showed the world who you were becoming.

I was in grade school, but I already knew something most adults were still figuring out: *clothes tell stories before you ever open your mouth.*

My outfit that day wasn't bought off a rack. It was *designed*. A custom denim rhinestone airbrushed jacket with the entire city of Philadelphia sprawling across my back— the skyline, the pride, the grit, the glory. Ripped denim jeans that said I wasn't trying too hard but still cared. And mustard yellow Reebok high-top snaps that tied it all together like a bow on a gift nobody asked for, but everybody wanted.

I didn't just get dressed that morning. I *built* an outfit. I represented my city in the best light I could imagine, using the only tools I had: my mind, my creativity, and my love for where I'm from.

This wasn't about West Philadelphia born and raised like the Fresh Prince. This was deeper. This was *intentional*. This was the moment I realized fashion wasn't just about looking good—it was about making people *feel* something when they saw you.

That Easter Sunday, I cracked a code I didn't even know existed.

And even though life tried to bury it, even though the streets tried to steal it, even though I almost lost it twice—that code never left me.

WHY THIS BOOK EXISTS

This book isn't for everyone. And that's the first truth I need you to understand.

Not everyone can do this. Not everyone *should* do this. Styling isn't just about liking clothes or following trends on Instagram. It's about having the *heart* for fashion, the *mind* for creativity, the *eye* for what works, and the *skill* to bring it all together in a way that transforms people.

If you're reading this, you're one of two people:

You're the dreamer. You've always had a heart for fashion. You see an outfit in your head before it exists. You watch people walk by and mentally redesign their look. You know you were made for this, but you don't know where to start. You're standing at the edge, holding onto a thread, wondering if it's strong enough to pull you into the life you were meant to live.

Or...

You're the stuck stylist. You've been in the industry, but you've hit a wall. You're talented, but you're not booked. You're creative, but you're not getting paid what you're worth. You know there's a code to this game, but you haven't cracked it yet. You're frustrated, maybe even thinking about giving up.

I've been both.

This book is the thread. It's the hem of the garment. It's the thing you reach for when everything else has failed.

x

I'm writing this because I know what it's like to have a dream buried under life's chaos. I know what it's like to hold onto something so tightly that your hands hurt, even when you can't see the finish line. And I know what it's like to finally crack the code and realize: *this was always meant for me.*

If you've got the heart, the mind, the eye, and the willingness to build the skill—this book will show you how to crack the code.

Hold on tight.

Let's get started.

PART ONE

KNOW YOUR LANE

The Three Categories That Will Define Your Career

Before you can crack the code, you need to know what game you're playing.

Too many aspiring stylists make the mistake of thinking they can do it all. They want to style everyone, for every occasion, in every genre. That's not a business strategy—that's a recipe for burnout and confusion.

The truth is, the stylists who make it big, who build recognizable brands, who get booked solid and paid what they're worth, are the ones who picked a lane and mastered it first.

There are three main categories in the styling world, and you need to figure out which one speaks to your soul before you ever touch a client:

1. **Urban/Streetwear** - The Culture

2. **Business/Formal Wear** - The Power Look

3. **Haute Formal** - The Statement Pieces

Let me break down each one so you can figure out where you belong.

Category 1: Urban/Streetwear – The Culture Speaks

This is where fashion meets identity. Urban and streetwear isn't just about hoodies, joggers, sneakers, and distressed denim—it's about representing a culture, a movement, a moment in time.

Think about it: when you see someone rocking a fresh pair of Air Jordans with ripped jeans, an oversized graphic tee, and a fitted cap, you're not just seeing clothes. You're seeing a statement.

You're seeing someone who knows the culture, respects the origins, and understands that streetwear is rooted in hip-hop, skateboarding, and urban communities that turned limited resources into limitless creativity.

Who thrives in this category:

- Stylists who grew up in the culture and can speak its language authentically

- People who know the difference between wearing Supreme and *understanding* Supreme

- Creatives who can blend high-end designers (like Off-White, Fear of God, Yeezy) with accessible brands (like Nike, Adidas, Champion) and make it look effortless

- Stylists who understand that a fresh pair of sneakers can make or break an entire outfit

Common pieces in this category:

- Sneakers (Jordans, Yeezys, Dunks, Air Force 1s)

- Hoodies and crewneck sweatshirts

- Joggers, cargo pants, distressed denim

- Graphic tees with cultural relevance

- Oversized outerwear (bombers, puffer jackets, windbreakers)

- Fitted caps, beanies, bucket hats

- Accessories: chains, watches, bags (crossbody, backpacks)

Your clientele:

- Young professionals who want to look fresh but still polished

- Creatives, artists, musicians, influencers

- Athletes in their off-duty looks

- Anyone who wants to feel connected to the pulse of what's current

Urban/streetwear is about knowing what's dropping before it drops. It's about understanding limited releases, collaboration culture, and the stories behind the brands. If you can tell someone why a pair of Travis Scott Jordans matters beyond just the price tag, you might belong here.

But here's the reality check: if you didn't grow up in this world, if you're just chasing trends without understanding the roots, your clients will know.

Authenticity is everything in streetwear. You can't fake this lane.

Category 2: Business/Formal Wear – The Power Look

This is the category that built my career. And let me tell you something: people underestimate the power of a well-fitted suit until they put one on and feel the shift in how they carry themselves.

Business and formal wear isn't about being boring or "corporate." It's about confidence. It's about walking into a room and commanding respect before you say a word. It's about understanding that the way you present yourself in professional spaces can open doors or close them.

Who thrives in this category:

- Stylists who understand tailoring and fit (this is NON-NEGOTIABLE)

- People who can read a room and dress someone appropriately for the occasion

- Creatives who know how to add personality to a suit without making it costumey

- Stylists who can work with different body types and make everyone feel powerful

Common pieces in this category:

- Tailored suits (two-piece, three-piece)

- Dress shirts and blouses

- Slacks, dress pants, pencil skirts

- Blazers and sport coats

- Dress shoes (Oxfords, loafers, heels, pumps)

- Ties, bow ties, pocket squares

- Professional dresses and coordinate sets

- Accessories: watches, cufflinks, structured bags

Your clientele:

- Executives, entrepreneurs, corporate professionals

- People preparing for interviews, board meetings, speaking engagements

- Young professionals building their image

- Anyone transitioning from casual to corporate environments

Here's what most people don't understand about business and formal wear: it's not just about putting someone in a suit. It's about understanding *their* power and helping them project it.

When I started styling in this category, I thought my audience was going to be church folks. I loved the idea of helping people show up to service looking sharp, feeling confident, and representing well. That made sense to me because of my roots and where I came from.

But that's not where my business took off.

I'll tell you more about that in Part Two, but here's the lesson: just because you *think* you know your audience doesn't mean you actually do.

Sometimes the market will show you where you belong, and you have to be flexible enough to follow it.

Category 3: Haute Formal – The Statement Pieces

This is the top tier. This is where fashion becomes art. This is tuxedos with custom beading, ball gowns with hand-stitched embellishments, three-piece suits with luxury fabrics, and accessories that cost more than most people's rent.

Haute formal is not for the faint of heart. This is where you work with clients who have specific visions, high expectations, and the budget to make it happen. This is red carpets, galas, high-society weddings, and once-in-a-lifetime events.

Who thrives in this category:

- Stylists with an eye for luxury and detail

- People who understand fabric quality, construction, and couture

- Creatives who can source rare pieces or work with custom designers

- Stylists who can handle high-pressure, high-stakes events

Common pieces in this category:

- Custom tuxedos and tailcoats
- Ball gowns and evening dresses
- Luxury fabrics (silk, velvet, satin, brocade)
- Statement jewelry (diamonds, custom pieces)
- Designer shoes (Louboutin, Jimmy Choo, Tom Ford)
- High-end accessories (clutches, cufflinks, capes, gloves)
- Embellishments (beading, rhinestones, embroidery, sequins)

Your clientele:

- Celebrities, entertainers, public figures
- High-net-worth individuals attending exclusive events
- Brides and grooms with luxury wedding budgets
- Clients attending galas, award shows, or charity events

This category requires connections. You need to know designers, boutiques, and tailors who can execute at the highest level. You need to understand how to style someone so they stand out but don't look overdone. And you need to be comfortable working with clients who have strong opinions and big personalities.

If you can master haute formal, you'll never struggle to find work. But it takes years of building your reputation, your network, and your portfolio before you can charge what this level demands.

Finding Your Category: The Honest Assessment

Now that you've seen the three main categories, here's the question you need to answer:

Which one feels like home?

Not which one seems the most profitable. Not which one your friends think you should do. Not which one looks cool on Instagram.

Which one makes you feel something when you think about it?

Because here's the truth: you can learn the skills for any of these categories.

You can study fabrics, practice tailoring, research trends, and build your technical knowledge. But you can't fake passion. You can't fake authenticity. And you can't build a sustainable career in a lane that doesn't align with who you are.

When I think about business and formal wear, I feel something. I see my clients walking into rooms with their shoulders back, their heads high, knowing they look like the powerful person they're becoming. That's what drives me. That's my lane.

What's yours?

Ask yourself:

- What kind of styling gets you excited when you see it in the wild?
- What category do you naturally gravitate toward when you're shopping for yourself?

- What events or occasions do you wish you could style for?

- Where do you feel most confident in your knowledge and taste?

Once you know your category, everything else gets easier. Your branding gets clearer. Your target audience becomes more defined. Your portfolio becomes more cohesive. And most importantly, you stop trying to be everything to everyone and start becoming the go-to expert in your lane.

Need help figuring out your category or refining your vision? That's exactly what I help stylists do. Reach out at stylesbycheydesigns@gmail.com or visit stylesbycheydesigns.com to learn more about my consulting services.

KNOW YOUR AUDIENCE (OR BUILD ONE)

The Audience Isn't Always Who You Think

Let me tell you about the biggest mistake I made when I started my styling career.

I thought I knew exactly who my audience was. I had it all figured out. I was going to style people in business and formal wear, specifically for church. It made perfect sense to me. I came from the church. I understood the culture. I knew that people wanted to look their best on Sunday mornings. I knew the importance of representing well in the house of God.

So I marketed to churches. I reached out to pastors, deacons, choir members, and church leadership. I created content around looking sharp for service. I built my messaging around dignity, respect, and showing up powerfully for worship.

And you know what happened?

Not much.

Don't get me wrong—I got a few clients here and there. But it wasn't the wave I thought it was going to be. It wasn't the boom. It wasn't the breakthrough.

I was frustrated. I was confused. I had the skills, I had the passion, I had the category locked in. So what was I missing?

Here's what I learned: **just because you think you know your audience doesn't mean you actually do.**

The market will tell you where you belong. And if you're smart, you'll listen.

My Church Wasn't My Audience—My Proms Were

The turning point came in 2017.

A client walked into my life with a vision that would change everything. She was planning prom, and she had a theme that sounded almost impossible: **"Dubai to North Philly."**

She wanted three custom suits. Not just any suits—she wanted something that would capture the opulence of Dubai while honoring the grit and pride of North Philadelphia. She had a creative mind. I had a creative mind. And when two creative minds come together with a shared vision, magic happens.

I didn't know it then, but those three suits were about to break the internet.

When prom night arrived and the photos dropped, the response was immediate. Not just local buzz—*global* recognition. Good Morning America. Fox News. CBS. NBC. Every major news outlet was covering it. The theme "Dubai to North Philly" didn't just trend in Philadelphia—it reached *actual Dubai*. What started in West Philly went global.

Overnight, I went from stylist to **celebrity stylist.**

Before that prom, I had about 8,000 followers on social media. I was posting church looks, formal wear, building slowly. After that prom? I gained over 20,000 new followers almost instantly. My DMs exploded. My phone wouldn't stop ringing. I wasn't just in demand in Philly anymore—I was being contacted by clients across the country, across the world.

That small thread I'd been holding onto for years? It suddenly unrolled into the entire spool.

This was my aha moment becoming reality. The dream I'd seen on Easter Sunday 1990 was now playing out on a stage bigger than I ever imagined.

The audience I thought I was serving (the church) wasn't where my business was going to explode. The audience that actually needed me, that was willing to invest, that was going to elevate my brand and take me global, was the **prom market**.

And once I leaned into that, everything changed.

Building vs. Finding: The Reality Check

Here's the hard truth that no one tells you when you're starting out: sometimes you don't *find* your audience. You *build* it.

But sometimes? Sometimes you create something so undeniable that the audience finds *you*.

That 2017 prom wasn't just a job. It was a statement. It was proof that when you execute at the highest level, when you bring someone's vision to life in a way that makes people stop scrolling and pay attention, the world will notice.

I didn't have a marketing budget. I didn't run ads. I didn't have a PR team.

What I had was work that spoke for itself.

When those photos hit social media, they went viral. News outlets picked it up. Blogs wrote about it. People shared it across platforms. And suddenly, I wasn't chasing clients anymore—they were chasing me.

But here's what made that moment possible: I didn't treat it like "just another prom." I treated it like the opportunity of a lifetime. Because that's what it turned out to be.

That client came to me with a creative vision, and instead of just executing it, I *elevated* it. I brought my own creativity to the table. I pushed the boundaries. I made sure every detail was perfect. I didn't just give her what she asked for—I gave her something unforgettable.

And that's the lesson: **you don't know which project is going to be the one that changes everything, so you have to treat every single one like it is.**

Here's what building (and exploding) an audience actually looks like:

1. **Start with excellence, not exposure.**

    Don't focus on going viral. Focus on doing work so good that people can't help but talk about it. The exposure will follow.

2. **Say yes to creative challenges.**

    That Dubai to North Philly concept could've felt risky. It could've felt too ambitious. But I leaned in. I trusted the vision. And it paid off in ways I couldn't have imagined.

3. **Document everything.**

    Those prom photos didn't just exist in person—they were captured professionally, shared intentionally, and spread like wildfire because the visuals were undeniable.

4. **Be ready when the moment comes.**

    When Good Morning America called, I didn't freeze. When my DMs flooded, I responded. When opportunities showed up, I was prepared to seize them.

5. **Lean into what works.**

    After that prom went viral, I didn't go back to only posting church looks. I doubled down on proms, formals, and high-impact styling. That's where the demand was, so that's where I focused.

    I could've fought the fact that proms became my lane. I could've insisted that church styling was my calling and ignored what the market was showing me. But I would've missed the breakthrough.

Instead, I listened. I leaned in. I became known as the stylist who could turn a prom into a global moment. And once I owned that reputation, my business exploded.

That small thread I'd been holding onto since Easter Sunday 1990? It unrolled into an entire career. A brand. A movement.

From West Philly to the world.

The One Client That Changes Everything

Let me tell you something that might sound dramatic, but it's the absolute truth: **You are always one client away from your breakthrough.**

One client away from the project that goes viral. One client away from the recognition that puts you on the map. One client away from the moment that takes you from local to global.

But here's the catch: you won't know which client it is until after the fact.

That 2017 prom client who came to me with the "Dubai to North Philly" vision? I had no idea she was going to be the catalyst for everything. I didn't know those three suits would be photographed and shared millions of times. I didn't know Good Morning America would cover it. I didn't know I'd gain 20,000+ followers overnight. I didn't know it would take my West Philly brand global.

I just showed up. I listened to her vision. I brought my creativity to the table. I executed at the highest level. And it changed everything.

That's why you have to treat every single client, every single job, every single request like it's the one that's going to change everything.

Because it might be.

Are You Ready? Treating Every Opportunity Like It's THE One

Most stylists fail not because they lack talent. They fail because they're inconsistent.

They give 100% to the client who's paying top dollar, but they phone it in for the client who's on a budget. They show up fully for the high-profile event, but they're distracted and rushed for the "small" job.

That's how you stay stuck.

Here's the mindset shift that will change your career: **Every client is your audition for the next level.**

That means:

- You're never "too good" for a job

- You never cut corners because someone isn't paying you what you think you're worth

- You show up on time, prepared, and professional every single time

- You communicate clearly, set expectations, and follow through

- You make every client feel like they're your only client

When you operate like this, two things happen:

1. **You build an unshakeable reputation.**

   People talk. Word spreads. When your name comes up, it's always followed by praise. "They're the best." "They never disappoint." "You have to work with them."

2. **You attract better opportunities.**

High-quality clients don't just appear out of no-where. They come through referrals from other high-quality clients. And those referrals only happen when you've proven that you're worth recommending.

I'm going to say it one more time because it's that important:

You are only one client away from everything changing.

Are you ready?

Are you showing up like you believe that?

Or are you treating this like a side hustle, a hobby, some-thing you'll get serious about "one day"?

Because the stylists who make it—who crack the code, who build thriving businesses, who get to do this full-time and actually make money—are the ones who treated it like their life depended on it from day one.

Not because they were desperate. But because they were *committed*.

PART THREE

MAKE IT OFFICIAL—BUILDING THE FOUNDATION

Why You Need More Than Talent to Be Taken Seriously

Let me be blunt: talent is not enough.

You can have the best eye for style in your city. You can put together outfits that make people stop and stare. You can have clients who love you and swear by your work.

But if you're not operating as a legitimate business, you're limiting yourself in ways you don't even realize.

Here's what happens when you're just "doing styling on the side" without making it official:

- You can't write off your expenses

- You can't build business credit

- You can't open a business bank account

- You can't get wholesale pricing from vendors

- You struggle to get taken seriously by event planners, photographers, and other industry professionals

- You can't scale beyond word-of-mouth referrals

And worst of all? You're leaving money on the table.

When I finally made the decision to formalize my business—to stop operating under the table and start operating like a real company—everything shifted. Clients started taking me more seriously. Vendors started offering me better deals. My income increased. My opportunities expanded.

But more than that, *I* started taking myself more seriously.

Because when you make it official, you're not just telling the world you're in business. You're telling yourself: *I'm not playing anymore. This is real.*

The Business Essentials: EIN, LLC, Seller's Permit

Let's break down what you actually need to establish your styling business legally and professionally.

1. **EIN (Employer Identification Number)**

   This is your business's social security number. You need it to open a business bank account, file taxes, and establish your business as a separate entity from your personal finances.

The good news? It's free to get. You can apply for an EIN directly through the IRS website, and you'll get it instantly.

Why you need it:

- Separates your personal and business finances

- Required to open a business bank account

- Necessary if you ever want to hire employees or contractors

- Makes you look legitimate when working with vendors and clients

2. LLC (Limited Liability Company)

An LLC protects you personally if something goes wrong in your business. If a client sues you, if you go into debt, if something happens—your personal assets (your house, your car, your personal bank account) are protected. It also gives you credibility. When clients see "Stylesbychey, LLC" instead of just "Cheynne Smith," they know you're serious.

Why you need it:

- Legal protection for your personal assets

- Tax benefits (you can write off business expenses)

- Professional credibility

- Easier to scale and grow

How to set it up: You can file for an LLC through your state's Secretary of State website. The process varies by state, but it's usually straightforward. In most states, the filing fee is between $50-$500.

If the paperwork feels overwhelming, don't let that stop you. **I help entrepreneurs set up their LLCs, get their EINs, and handle all the business formation details so they can focus on their craft.**

Visit stylesbycheydesigns.com or call me at 856.656.8202 to learn more.

3. **Seller's Permit (depending on your state)**

   If you're selling physical products—clothing, accessories, or styling packages that include items you purchase and resell—you may need a seller's permit (also called a sales tax permit or resale certificate).

This allows you to:

- Collect sales tax from clients (if required in your state)
- Purchase inventory wholesale without paying sales tax upfront
- Operate legally as a retail business

Not every stylist needs this. If you're only charging for your time and expertise (like consultation fees or styling services), you probably don't. But if you're putting together looks and marking up the clothing, you likely do.

Check your state's requirements. Some states are strict about this. Don't skip this step.

Opening Your Business Bank Account

Once you have your EIN and LLC, your next move is opening a business bank account.

This is non-negotiable.

Why you need a separate business account:

- Keeps your personal and business finances separate (critical for taxes)

- Makes you look professional when clients see payments going to your business name

- Helps you track income and expenses accurately

- Required if you want to build business credit

What you'll need to open an account:

- Your EIN

- Your LLC formation documents

- A government-issued ID

- An initial deposit (usually $25-$100)

Most banks offer free business checking accounts for small businesses. Shop around. Look for accounts with low fees, easy online banking, and good customer service.

And here's a pro tip: once you open your business account, *only* use it for business. Don't mix personal expenses in there. Keep it clean. This will make your life so much easier when tax season comes.

Building Business Credit from Day One

Here's something most new business owners don't think about: your business can have its own credit score, separate from your personal credit.

And if you build it right, you can use your business credit to:

- Get business loans
- Finance equipment or inventory
- Get business credit cards with better terms
- Establish yourself as a credible, stable business

How to start building business credit:

1. **Get a DUNS number**

   This is a free business identification number from Dun & Bradstreet. It's like a social security number for your business. Apply at dnb.com.

2. **Open trade lines with vendors**

   Work with vendors who report to business credit bureaus. Pay your invoices on time. This builds your credit history.

3. **Get a business credit card**

   Use it for business expenses and pay it off every month. This shows you can manage credit responsibly.

4. **Pay everything on time**

   Late payments hurt your business credit just like they hurt your personal credit.

Be consistent.

Building business credit takes time, but if you start now, you'll thank yourself in two years when you need financing to scale.

Creating Your Brand Identity: Logo & Presence

Your business isn't just about paperwork. It's about perception.

When someone hears your name, what do they think? When they see your logo, what do they feel? When they visit your website or social media, what impression do they get?

This is your brand identity, and it matters more than you think.

You need:

1. **A professional logo**

   Not something you threw together on Canva in 10 minutes. A real logo that represents who you are and what you do. If you can't design it yourself, hire a graphic designer. It's worth the investment.

2. A cohesive color scheme

Pick 2-3 colors that represent your brand and stick with them. Use them in your logo, your website, your social media graphics, your business cards. Consistency builds recognition.

3. A clear brand voice

Are you fun and edgy? Professional and polished? Bold and confident? Figure out your voice and make sure it comes through in everything you post and say.

4. High-quality visuals

Invest in good photos of your work. Before-and-afters. Styled looks. Client testimonials with faces. Your portfolio is your proof. Make it undeniable.

Need help building your brand from scratch? I offer full brand development services, from logo design to social media strategy. Reach out at stylesbycheydesigns@gmail.com.

The Network Effect: Why Who You Know Matters

Let me tell you something that might sound harsh: your skill will only get you so far. Your network will take you the rest of the way.

The stylists who are booked solid aren't necessarily the most talented. They're the most *connected.*

They know event planners who refer them to clients. They know photographers who tag them in posts. They know boutique owners who recommend them to shoppers. They know other stylists who send overflow work their way.

Building a network isn't about being fake or using people. It's about creating genuine relationships with people in your industry who can help you grow—and who you can help in return.

Here's how to build your network:

1. **Show up to industry events**

   Fashion shows, trunk shows, networking mixers, trade shows. Go. Introduce yourself. Exchange contact info. Follow up.

2. **Collaborate with other creatives**

   Photographers, makeup artists, hairstylists, event planners. Do styled shoots together. Cross-promote each other. Build a team.

3. **Join online communities**

   Facebook groups, Instagram communities, LinkedIn groups for stylists and fashion professionals. Engage. Share your work. Be helpful.

4. **Support other people's work**

   Comment on their posts. Share their content. Celebrate their wins. When you lift others up, they'll lift you up too.

5. Be someone people want to work with

Show up on time. Communicate clearly. Be professional. Be kind. Your reputation will follow you everywhere. Your network is your net worth. Build it intentionally.

Social Media: Your Digital Storefront

Let's be real: if you're not on social media in 2025, you don't exist to most potential clients.

Instagram, TikTok, Facebook—these aren't just fun apps. They're your portfolio, your marketing team, and your sales funnel all rolled into one.

Here's what your social media should do:

1. Show your work

Post styled looks regularly. Before-and-afters. Behind-the-scenes. Client testimonials.

2. **Educate your audience**

    Share styling tips. Talk about fabrics, fits, and trends. Position yourself as the expert.

3. **Build trust**

    Show your face. Share your story. Let people see the person behind the brand.

4. **Drive action**

    Include clear calls-to-action. "DM me to book." "Link in bio for consultations." Make it easy for people to work with you.

You don't need to post 10 times a day. But you do need to be consistent. Pick a schedule you can actually stick to and show up.

And here's the key: quality over quantity. One incredible post that shows your skill and tells a story is worth more than 10 mediocre posts.

Struggling with social media strategy? I help stylists build their online presence and turn followers into paying clients. Let's talk: stylesbycheydesigns.com | 856.656.8202

FROM CRACKING THE CODE
TO BREAKING THE CODE

Here's what we've covered in this book:

- ☑ You know your category (Urban, Business/Formal, or Haute Formal)
- ☑ You understand that your audience might not be who you think—and that's okay
- ☑ You're treating every client like they're the one that will change everything
- ☑ You've made your business official with an EIN, LLC, and all the legal foundations
- ☑ You're building your brand, your network, and your social media presence

You've cracked the code.

But here's the thing: cracking the code is just the beginning.

Once you know the rules, once you understand the game, the next step is learning how to *break* the code. How to scale beyond yourself. How to charge premium prices. How to build a team. How to turn your styling business into a brand that lasts.

That's what we'll cover in **Book 2: *Breaking the Style Code.***

But before we get there, I need you to do something:

Take action on what you just learned.

Don't just read this book and put it down.

Don't just get inspired and then go back to scrolling Instagram.

Crack the code. Make it official. Start building.

Because the industry is waiting for you. Your clients are out there. Your breakthrough is one decision, one client, one bold move away.

And when you're ready to take it to the next level—when you're ready to not just crack the code, but break it wide open—I'll be here.

Let's build this together.

Connect with Cheyenne:
Website: stylesbycheydesigns.com
Email: stylesbycheydesigns@gmail.com

Instagram: @stylesbychey
Phone: 856.656.8202

Coming Soon: Book 2 - Breaking the Style Code
The Style Code Series continues...